PARABLE PRAISE PARTY

COME BACK HOME

written by Mary Rice Hopkins

illustrated by Dennas Davis

Faith Parenting Guide

Ages 4-7

Holiness

FaithKidz®

A Faith Parenting Guide can be found on page 35.

Faith Kidz is an imprint of Cook Communications Ministries
Colorado Springs, Colorado 80918
Cook Communications, Paris, Ontario
Kingsway Communications, Eastbourne, England

First printing, 2004
Printed in the United States.

1 2 3 4 5 6 7 8 9 10 Printing/Year 08 07 06 05 04

ISBN: 0781439914

Editor: Heather Gemmen
Interior Designer: Granite Design

To my three brothers, Wayne, Jimmy and Joe
whom I love dearly. — MRH

For Ruthie — DD

Once there were two sons and a dad who loved them so.
But one son said, "I'm out of here."
He said, "I want to go."

"Please give me what is mine, and I'll party with my friends. I want to see what I can buy. I want to spend and spend."

So he turned to go away with just a quick goodbye. The father was so very sad. A tear came to his eye.

8

9

The young man left without a thought to things he left behind.
He just thought of what he'd do and all the fun he'd find.
He laughed and partied all night long
and slept through all the day...

See the Big Dogs

40

And so he finally thought about all he'd left back home
Life was better with his dad when he was not alone.

He said, "I wish I didn't leave that dear old dad of mine.
I wouldn't be eating with the pigs and living with the swine."

17

"I'll ask my dad if I can be just like his hired hand.
His servants have a better life. I'll hope he'll understand."

19

So he left to go back home to say sorry to his dad. "I'll ask for his forgiveness. I wonder if he's mad."

The father saw him coming, and he ran out of the door.
He gave the son some presents;
but his words meant so much more.

24

The father said, "I love you, son.
You were lost, but now you're found.
It's time to eat the fatted cow
with everyone in town."

The father was so happy and thankful for his son. He said, "Come on, let's celebrate all that God has done."

Jesus said,

"There was a man who had two sons. The younger one said to his father, 'Father, give me my share of the estate.' So he divided his property between them.

Not long after that, the younger son got together all he had, set off for a distant country and there squandered his wealth in wild living. After he had spent everything, there was a severe famine in that whole country, and he began to be in need. So he went and hired himself out to a citizen of that country, who sent him to his fields to feed pigs. He longed to fill his stomach with the pods that the pigs were eating, but no one gave him anything.

When he came to his senses, he said, 'How many of my father's hired men have food to spare, and here I am starving to death! I will set out and go back to my father and say to him: Father, I have sinned against heaven and against you. I am no longer worthy to be called your son; make me like one of your hired men.' So he got up and went to his father. But while he was still a long way off, his father saw him and was filled with compassion for him; he ran to his son, threw his arms around him and kissed him. The son said to him, 'father, I have sinned against heaven and against you. I am no longer worthy to be called your son.'

But the father said to his servants, 'Quick! Bring the best robe and put it on him. Put a ring on his finger and sandals on his feet. Bring the fattened calf and kill it. Let's have a feast and celebrate. For this son of mine was dead and is alive again; he was lost and is found.' So they began to celebrate."

Luke 15:11–24

Come On Home

Words & Music by
Mary Rice Hopkins

Country swing feel: ♩ = 110

1st verse

I've got two sons___ As dif-f'rent as___ can be Both of them___ are spe - cial

In our___ fam - i - ly   One of them___ he works so hard And helps us in our home   The

oth - er was dis-sat-is-fied And said I want to   roam___ I want to roam   Well

I was sad___ when he said Dad__ I just want my mon-ey So he took his in-her-it-ance___ And

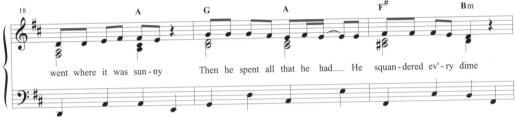

went where it was sun-ny Then he spent all that he had___ He squan-dered ev'-ry dime

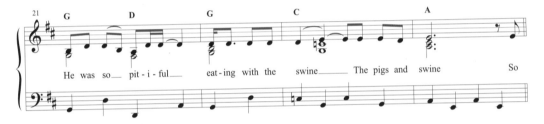

He was so___ pit-i-ful___ eat-ing with the swine_____ The pigs and swine So

chorus

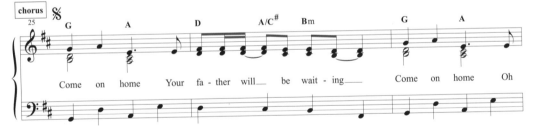

Come on home Your fa-ther will___ be wait-ing___ Come on home Oh

we're an-tic-i-pat-ing___ Come on home Turn a-round and change your ways 'Cause your

dad won't_ be mad   In   fact he'll_ be glad   Your   dad won't_ be mad   When

you   come   home

3rd/4th verse

Then he   saw his fool-ish ways_ And   re-turned to the farm   My   heart_   leapt for joy_   And I
Then   I   placed a gold-en   ring   Up - on_   his   hand   We   danced and sang all_   night_   And

o - pened   up   the   barn   Then we   ate   the fat-ted   cow_ With   ev'ry-one_   a-round   My
played_   with the band   My   son_   said I   love you dad_   I'll   nev-er   leave   a-gain   Your

son   had_   been lost   But   now   he's been   found_   He's   been   found

32

for-give-ness has brought me home____ You are__ my friend__ my best__ friend So

CODA

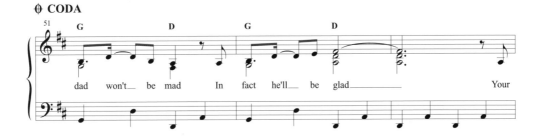

dad won't__ be mad In fact he'll__ be glad_____ Your

dad won't__ be mad When you come home You come on home

Come on home

33

Come On Home

I've got two sons
As different as can be
Both of them are special
In our family
One of them he works so hard
And helps us in our home
The other was dissatisfied
And said I want to roam
I want to roam

Well I was sad when he said Dad
I just want my money
So he took his inheritance
And went where it was sunny
Then he spent all that he had
He squandered every dime
He was so pitiful eating with the swine
The pigs and swine

Chorus
(So) Come on home
Your father will be waiting
Come on home
Oh we're anticipating
Come on home
Turn around and change your ways
'Cause your dad won't be mad
In fact he'll be glad
Your dad won't be mad
When you come home

Then he saw his foolish ways
And returned to the farm
My heart leapt for joy
And I opened up the barn
Then we ate the fatted cow
With everyone around
My son had been lost
But now he's been found
He's been found

Then I placed a golden ring
upon his hand
We danced and sang all night
and played with the band
My son said I love you dad
I'll never leave again
Your forgiveness has brought me home
You are my friend my best friend

COME BACK HOME

Ages: 4-7

Life Issue: I want my children to walk in step with the Spirit.

Spiritual Building Block: Holiness

Do the following sight activities to help your children understand God's care for them:

Sight: Invite your kids to act out the story of the lost son. Gather props together to make a highly visual production: collect stuffed animals for pigs, wrap empty boxes for presents, make a crown out of tinfoil, use a bathrobe for a robe, create yummy snacks for the party. Play different roles together so your kids can experience both sides: loving a lost one and being loved. Tell your kids to show the emotions on their faces: the father's delight and the son's thankfulness.

Then act out the story with different endings: Have the father be angry at the son and not let the son back home. Or have the son decide not to go home. Tell your kids to show the emotions with their faces: the father's anger or sadness and the son's hurt or pride.

Ask your kids which story they liked best and which facial expressions they were most happy about. Tell them that God loves us and wants to welcome us back when we go away from him. He won't cross his arms and be angry at us if we come back to him. He will run out to meet us, like he did in the first story.

Sound: Gather a bunch of kids together and read the book to them. Then tell them you want to play a game with them:

Ask one child to volunteer to leave the room for a moment.

Choose another child to volunteer to say the name of the child who left the room out loud when that child returns.

Call the first child back in the room. Ask him or her to turn away from the other kids and to listen very closely.

After the second child says the name, invite the first child to guess who said it.

Play the game a few times or until everyone has had a chance to participate in both roles. Then tell the kids to tell you how they knew who called their name. When they realize that they recognized the voice because they know the other child, tell them that we can get to know God so well that we can recognize his voice as well. We may hear his voice in ways that are different from hearing our friends—through prayer, when a parent or teacher or pastor tells us something, when our hearts connect with a scripture passage—but it is still God's voice speaking to us.

Assure the kids that God loves us very much and has very good plans for us.

 Touch: Place footsteps on the floor and have your children follow them to different destinations: lead them to a lovely picture on the wall for them to look at, lead them to the garbage can so they can empty the trash, lead them to the telephone to so they can call a friend, lead them to the play dough so they can use their skills to make something.

Talk about how God leads us to different places and through various events in our lives. He takes us places, but it is up to us to respond appropriately. We can respond with obedience and so enjoy what he gives us, or we can ignore him and so never fully enjoy his plan for us.

Pair up your children. Blindfold one child and have the other lead the first one through an obstacle course.

Talk about how we have to trust God to lead us even when we have no idea where he is leading us. And tell them that we can dare to trust God because he loves us so much.